Time Management

Numerous Strategies To Enhance Productivity And Attain Superior Outcomes With Reduced Exertion, Reclaim Your Time And Rediscover The Joys Of Life

(Strategies For Enhancing Productivity, Time Management, And Conquering Procrastination)

Alberto Taylor

TABLE OF CONTNET

Individual Evaluation 1

Establishing Priorities And Objectives 7

Creating Intentional Objectives 13

Self-Help Tips 27

Handling Diversion 45

Typical Workplace Diversions 45

An Overview Of Time Management For Entrepreneurs 61

Accepting Change 86

Instruments For Assessment And Modification 98

Explore The Psychological Underpinnings Of Why Humans Procrastinate 110

Time Theft: The Effects Of Postponement 128

Individual Evaluation

Self-awareness and Introspection

One of the most important steps in time management is self-evaluation.

Recognize your abilities, preferences, and behavioral tendencies before using management tactics and techniques.

In this process, introspection and self-awareness are crucial.

Spend some time thinking about your priorities, values, and objectives.

Techniques like journaling, meditation, or speaking with a coach or mentor can help you do this.

Using this self-assessment, you will be able to determine your areas of strength, difficulties, and room for improvement.

Determining the Advantages and Disadvantages

Following some initial introspection, it's critical to determine your time management strengths and shortcomings.

This will enable you to maximize your abilities and create plans for overcoming obstacles.

Examine your ability to focus, prioritize, plan, organize, and exercise self-control.

Think back to times when you felt effective and productive. Note the abilities that made such times possible. Then, think about how to use similar abilities in other aspects of your life.

Procrastination, trouble saying "no," an absence of organization, or a propensity for easily becoming distracted could be the cause.

Acknowledging these shortcomings will put you in a better position to develop tactics and solutions that work.

Define Improvement Goals

Establish time management improvement objectives based on your evaluation.

These goals should be time-bound, relevant, quantifiable, achievable, and targeted (SMART). Establish attainable objectives that tackle the primary areas you found in the self-evaluation that need work.

For instance, the aim can be to "Improve prioritization skill by identifying the most important tasks daily" if you've discovered that you struggle with task prioritization.

Creating Good Habits

After you've determined your improvement objectives, form virtuous habits that enhance your time management.

Recognize that while creating habits requires patience and perseverance, they can eventually result in big changes.

Make an action plan for every goal you have for progress.

If your objective is to increase self-control, schedule daily activities that support discipline. Some ideas for this include assigning specified times for tasks to be completed or utilizing reward systems to motivate goal attainment.

Adopt good habits like getting enough sleep, eating a balanced diet, and exercising; these will help you be a better time manager.

Observation and Modification

Finally, remember how crucial it is to monitor your time management process and modify your techniques as needed.

Regular self-evaluation and introspection can help you need to be tweaked.

Maintain a monitoring diary to log your everyday actions, assess your progress, and modify your strategies as necessary.

This will support sustained growth, motivation, and attention.

You must commit to implementing the ideas and tactics discussed in this chapter into your everyday life.

Recall that persistence and practice are necessary for efficient time management.

Here are some examples of how to apply what you've learned:

Decide to dedicate yourself to focusing on increasing your efficiency and managing your time better.

Although it will require work, the rewards will be worthwhile.

Implement the improvement objectives: Referring back to the improvement objectives you established in this chapter, begin their implementation.

Keep in mind that every goal needs to be tackled progressively and realistically.

Begin with minor adjustments, then move on to more difficult tasks as your confidence grows.

Make a plan of action: Create a precise and well-defined action plan for every improvement goal.

Put the actions you must conduct, the required materials, and the due dates you have established in writing.

Remember that having a well-organized plan will assist you in staying on course.

Track your development: Monitor your progress towards set targets regularly.

Celebrate your progress along the way and make modifications as necessary.

You may maintain your motivation and focus by continuously monitoring.

Ask for assistance and criticism: Look for outside assistance from a coach, mentor, or support group.

They can offer insightful advice, direction, and extra inspiration.

Sharing your path with others can also inspire and benefit from mutual learning.

Recall that time management is a continuous process of self-development.

Be willing to try new things, adjust to new situations, and learn from mistakes and accomplishments.

Creating a strong time management plan starts with a thorough personal assessment.

In the upcoming chapters, we'll look at goal-setting and prioritization techniques, action plan creation, and practice implementation to help you become a more proficient time manager.

I do not doubt that your actions will pay off for you.

Establishing Priorities And Objectives

The significance of well-defined objectives
For time management to be effective, goals must be clearly defined.

Setting and achieving goals gives your daily decisions and activities focus, direction, and a strong base.

This chapter will cover goal-setting techniques that are both relevant and practical.

SMART objectives

Using the SMART technique is a good way to set goals.

This acronym represents the five essential qualities that your objectives should have:

Particulars (Specific):

Your goals ought to be well-defined, exact, and unambiguous.

Steer clear of ambiguous goals because they can cause a lack of direction and attention.

Quantifiable (Quantifiable): Decide on precise standards to measure your development.

Establish quantifiable markers that let you keep track of your goals' progress.

Realistic: Make sure that your goals are attainable and reasonable given the circumstances.

When you set goals, consider your constraints, skills, and resources.

Relevant (Relevant): Your objectives should align with your long-term vision, priorities, and values.

Verify if they have significance and relevance for you.

Time-bound: Give yourself precise, measurable timeframes to meet your objectives.

This makes the work seem more urgent and holds you responsible for finishing it.

Setting Priorities

It's critical to prioritize and select the most critical and urgent tasks and activities and set clear objectives.

To assist you in this process, consider the following strategies:

The Eisenhower Matrix Sort your jobs into four quadrants using the Eisenhower matrix, sometimes called the urgency-importance matrix: important and urgent, important and not urgent, not important and urgent, and not important or urgent.

By doing this, you may prevent procrastination and focus on the most important activities.

Value Analysis: Assess each task's significance and worth in light of your aims and objectives.

Does this task make a major contribution to reaching my goals? If not, consider removing or assigning it to save time for more pertinent tasks.

Concentrate on the outcome: Prioritise outcomes and long-term effects.

Sort the tasks according to importance based on how they affect your objectives and desired results.

Establishing and Evaluating Priorities

Prioritization management is a continuous activity.

As new demands and situations emerge, you must constantly evaluate and revise your priorities.

The following advice will help you efficiently manage your priorities:

Regular Evaluation: Regularly assess your priorities by setting up time.

Depending on your circumstances and the demands of the moment, this could be done daily, weekly, or monthly.

Adaptability: Be willing to rearrange your priorities as necessary.

Unexpected events or fresh information can occasionally necessitate reevaluating and rearranging your workload.

Talking and Arranging:

Discussing your priorities and agreeing on deadlines and expectations with everyone involved is crucial if you work in a team or have shared duties.

By doing this, unneeded conflict is avoided, and everyone's priorities are in line.

Handling Too Much Work at Once

Having too many things to do is a regular occurrence in today's fast-paced environment.

The following are some useful tactics to assist you in meeting this challenge:

Transfer of authority: Determine which tasks can be assigned to resources or other individuals.

In addition to reducing your workload, delegation enables you to capitalize on the skills and talents of others.

Removing and Simplifying: Examine your activities regularly and cut out the ones that can be streamlined or don't add much to your goals.

Streamlining intricate activities can conserve both time and energy.

Learning to Say "No": Show the guts to turn down requests and assignments that don't fit into your priorities.

You can concentrate on your most significant objectives by concentrating on what matters most.

You'll take a significant step towards better time management by coordinating your activities with your top priorities.

In the upcoming chapters, we'll look at practical tools and strategic planning strategies to help you translate your objectives into actionable steps.

Prepare yourself to make a successful plan and establish ambitious targets.

Creating Intentional Objectives

We can more effectively manage our time and work towards our intended results with well-defined goals. To set significant goals, follow these steps:

1. Identify your mission: Your purpose is the first step towards creating meaningful goals. What goals do you have in mind? What is your ultimate objective? Determining your purpose clearly will assist you in establishing attainable objectives that complement your overarching vision.

2. Be Specific: Being precise while establishing goals is critical. Broad or ambiguous objectives might be challenging to accomplish and can not provide your actions with a clear direction. Instead, ensure your goals are clear, quantifiable, and easy to monitor and assess over time. For instance, make a goal like "run 5km in under 30 minutes by the end of the year" rather than just wanting to "get in shape."

3. Break down your objectives: Dividing your objectives into more manageable, smaller steps can increase their attainable nature and keep you engaged. Establish due dates for each of the precise steps to accomplish your goal. If your objective is to create a book, divide it into smaller tasks like creating chapter summaries, setting daily word counts, and editing each chapter.

4. Make your goals reasonable but demanding. Too simple or hard of a goal might deplete your motivation and cause dissatisfaction. Instead, make sure your goals are both ambitious and doable. Make goals that force you to step outside your comfort zone but are still attainable by considering your existing abilities and resources.

5. Put your goals in writing: It will help you keep them accountable and give them a more concrete sense. To monitor your progress, keep

your goals in a conspicuous location, like a vision board or planner, and review them frequently.

6. Celebrate your progress: Acknowledge and honor your advancement towards your objectives. No matter how tiny, celebrate your accomplishments and use them as fuel to keep going towards your bigger objectives.

To sum up, defining purposeful objectives is a critical component of efficient time management. You may position yourself for success and get the desired results by taking these simple actions.

Establishing Long-Term Goals

Setting meaningful goals and practicing efficient time management requires defining long-term objectives. Your long-term goals are the results you hope to get over an extended period, often one to five years. The following procedures can help you define your long-term goals:

1. Determine your vision: Your long-term goals should align with your life's overall vision. Think about your ideal life and your goals for the next several years. Think about your long-term objectives, passions, and values.

2. Specify your goals: After determining your vision, you should specify your long-term goals. They must be precise, quantifiable, and doable. Set a precise goal, such as "earn a promotion to a managerial position within five years," instead of a general one, like "be successful."

3. Make sure your goals and values line up: Make sure your long-term goals and values line up. You could find it difficult to maintain your motivation and dedication to reaching your goals if they contradict your moral principles.

4. Divide your main goals into more manageable ones: You can increase the attainableness of your long-term goals and maintain your motivation by breaking them

down into smaller goals. Establish due dates for each of the precise actions that must be taken to accomplish each goal.

5. Track your development: Regularly assess how well you achieve your long-term goals. Keep track of your accomplishments and modify your objectives as needed. Honor your successes and learn from your setbacks. Be adaptable: Be willing to modify your long-term goals in response to shifting priorities and situations. Because life is unpredictable, you may need to adjust your goals to take advantage of new possibilities or overcome new obstacles.

Establishing long-term goals is a crucial first step toward creating meaningful objectives and time management strategies. You may position yourself for success and attain your intended results by defining your vision, being adaptable, breaking your goals down into smaller goals, ensuring that they align with your values, tracking your progress, and keeping an eye on things.

Using Planners and To-Do Lists to Improve Time Management

Planners and to-do lists are useful tools for improving time management. Here's how they can assist you:

1. Prioritise your tasks: Making a planner or to-do list can assist you in focusing on and completing the most critical activities. Tasks can be arranged in order of significance or urgency, and you can approach them appropriately.

2. Maintain organization: By recording all the things you need to accomplish, a to-do list or planner can assist you in maintaining organization. By doing this, you may avoid forgetting crucial assignments or deadlines.

3. Lessen stress: Having a tonne of work to accomplish can be stressful and daunting. You can decrease stress and increase the sense of

accomplishment by breaking down jobs into smaller, more manageable chunks using a to-do list or planner.

4. Boost time management: By letting you project how long things will take and scheduling them appropriately, to-do lists and planners can help you better manage your time. Doing this may maximize your productivity and prevent squandering time on unimportant activities.

5. Boost productivity: You're more likely to be productive and succeed when you have a well-organized list of activities and a strategy for finishing them. As a result, you might feel more motivated and accomplished.

Here are some pointers for making efficient use of planners and to-do lists.

1. Keep things basic: Avoid piling too many tasks on your planner or to-do list. Keep things basic and concentrate on the most crucial task.

2. Be specific: Be clear about the tasks you need to do and the deadlines when adding them to your list. By doing this, you can ensure everything is finished on time and prevent confusion.

3. Review frequently: Check your calendar or to-do list frequently to ensure you're on track and make any necessary schedule adjustments.

4. Be adaptable: If unforeseen circumstances arise, be ready to modify your plans or reorder your priorities. You can avoid tension and frustration by doing this and maintaining your adaptability.

Using planners and to-do lists can help you stay organized, manage your time more effectively, lower stress levels, increase productivity, and accomplish your goals.

Benefits of Remote Work

The greatest benefit of working from home is having more time, which is why time management is crucial. Working from home has more advantages because you'll be more productive and have more time.

It Conserves Cash

Consider it. If you were not required to report to work each day? Transportation, meals, coffee, office attire, and snacks rapidly increase. The amount of money I spent on my daily coffee on the way to work was something I was unaware of. Most Americans are unaware that they might save anywhere from $1,000 to $2,000 annually if they stop purchasing coffee every morning (Rosen, 2020). Imagine the amount of money you could save by working from home, especially considering how much food and petrol currently cost. It is a significant benefit.

You Can Personalise Your Area

While working, we occasionally need a little consolation or motivation. This could take the shape of our all-time favorite sayings, keepsakes, tunes, or even pictures of the people we care about. An office or cubicle environment might not, however, permit such. It could make you uneasy to have your coworkers go through your belongings. Working from home allows you to personalize and design your workspace to your specifications!

Absence of Commuting

Indeed. This is how beneficial it is; therefore, I will say it again. One major benefit is not having to commute to work every day. You won't have to worry about waking up early or missing your appointment due to traffic, allowing you to get enough rest. In addition, your mood will lift in general. Furthermore, your and your company's carbon footprint is greatly reduced when you choose not to commute to work. Traffic reductions in cities worldwide have improved air quality and decreased greenhouse gas emissions!

Fewer Things to Stress Over

It feels wonderful to cross something off our to-do list when we have such hectic lifestyles. Imagine not needing to wake up early to get enough time to apply cosmetics or iron your clothes. These are not as big of a concern when you work from home. In addition, there are things like making it to your child's concert or stopping at the petrol station in the evening to avoid being late in the morning. You get a clearer schedule and a less busy mind when you eliminate the rush of travel time and irritated coworkers who won't let you work and work out when to fit in your workout. Less worries free up your thinking and make it easier to develop ideas. This has a profound impact on how you operate.

Improved Harmony between Work and Life

A clear work/life balance is possible if you work from home and set clear boundaries. You'll be able to find more time to work out, explore new interests, and spend more time with your loved ones. All of this helps you live a more balanced life rather than one where work takes up all of your energy.

Reduced Interruptions

It is simpler to become sidetracked or interrupted from work when you are at an office. Coworkers may be chatting loudly to one another, that they want to show you their new cat, or that you get sucked into a discussion about last night's football game. This reduces the time you can spend working and makes it harder to return to the flow state you were in before being interrupted. It may also be difficult for you to call clients; in this case, you must choose a quiet meeting space or go outside. Making phone calls is simpler, and these noisy distractions are eliminated when working from home.

Adaptable Timetable

You can have a flexible schedule if you work from home and use your time well. Supervisors typically don't mind if staff members leave for a meeting or pick up students from school as long as they can effectively manage their time and remain productive. This allows you extra time to complete tasks that you would typically try to fit into your weekends or assign to others. I've discovered that I can even work remotely while on the road with the right time management.

Self-Help Tips

For single mothers, incorporating self-help tips into their hectic lives is crucial. Self-help hacks offer invaluable resources to assist in managing the sometimes overwhelming demands of balancing motherhood, career, and personal wellbeing wellbeing.

With the help of the tips in this chapter, single mothers can prioritize their mental and emotional wellbeing, which improves their ability to handle stress and keep an optimistic outlook. Self-help hacks also provide lone mothers with techniques to increase resilience and self-worth.

Single mothers who look after themselves will be able to provide a good example for their kids and make sure they have the strength and stamina to give them the finest care possible.

Self-help tips are a lifeline for single mothers, supporting their general wellbeing and that of their families while assisting them in juggling the demands of single parenting.

Create a network of support.

Being a parent is a huge job that frequently calls for teamwork. Utilizing the different relationships in your life can create a new, strong support system, even if you don't have a typical nuclear family. Coworkers, friends, family, and loved ones are all part of this support system and can provide priceless help when needed.

Realize that there are people outside your immediate family in your support network. Think about friends who can offer emotional support, family members eager to assist, and coworkers who can assist on busy days. Family members concerned about your welfare might play a crucial role in your experience as a single mother.

Assign responsibilities to others to help spread the parenting load. Achieve greater independence in your kids by giving them age-appropriate responsibilities. This reduces your effort and helps your kids develop a sense of responsibility and independence.

Overcoming any guilt attached to asking for assistance is crucial. Most of the time, your friends, family, and coworkers are ready and willing to help you. With thanks, accept their help, understanding that it improves your family's quality of life.

Think about assigning chores to others and concentrating on your main competencies in your professional life. Communicate honestly and openly with your supervisor or employer to establish a work environment that is both balanced and supportive of your duties as a single mother.

Investigate the services and resources the community offers to help you handle your obligations. Arrange a carpool with other parents to avoid the early rush from school to work. You could also consider hiring a cleaning agency to tidy your house.

Hold the children's father responsible for whatever child support and help he has given or is expected to contribute, if relevant. Make sure all the preparations and communication are clear to satisfy your kids' needs.

Strong support systems reduce the strain and stress of being a single parent. Peace of mind comes from knowing you have trustworthy people to rely on when things get tough.

Single mothers may provide a caring atmosphere that supports their wellbeing and the development of their children by accepting the support and letting go of any guilt related to asking for assistance.

Make time for yourself.

Self-care frequently suffers in single-parent households because job and family life responsibilities collide. Prioritizing your family's needs makes perfect sense, especially if you provide most of the care.

But it's important to understand that putting off self-care will eventually make it more difficult to perform your duties well.

Basic needs like food, exercise, and sleep are all included in self-care. Ignoring these factors might sap your resilience and vitality, making it difficult to handle your many obligations.

It doesn't take a lot of time to practice self-care. The most notable results are frequently the result of modest, persistent efforts. For example, during your workday, set aside five minutes to meditate or take a few slow, deep breaths to help you center yourself. These attentive moments can assist you in recharging.

Include self-care in your family's everyday activities and routines, rather than seeing it as a solo project, including your kids or pets. Walking your dog or spending time outside with your children enhances family connection and is also good for your health.

Understand that caring for yourself doesn't have to be all you do. When you require some alone time, contact your support system. Don't be afraid to ask for help—whether with childcare or work-related obligations, ask relatives or friends for help.

You give your kids a good example and promote their wellbeing when you take good care of your own physical and mental health. Making self-care a priority helps you achieve a better work-life balance and increases your happiness.

You can work more productively and provide your family better care when you care for yourself. Self-care benefits you and your family by improving your energy, mental health, and general wellbeing.

What makes time management techniques crucial?

For many reasons, time management techniques are vital in our daily lives. We can enhance our emotional health, raise our productivity, and eventually improve the quality of our lives by comprehending and putting these strategies into practice. Here, we go into great detail about the significance of these tactics.

To begin with, effective time management raises production and efficiency. With so many things to do and so much information in today's fast-paced world, it's natural to feel overburdened. Time eludes us like water; most of the time, we feel like we haven't accomplished everything we set out to accomplish. By prioritizing and organizing our tasks, time management tactics enable us to do more in less time. These tactics include goal-setting, planning procedures, and methods for focusing and removing distractions.

Time management also helps us achieve a better work-life balance. Making efficient use of our time enables us to keep our personal and professional obligations apart, preventing one from invading the other. Knowing when to work and when to relax, committing ourselves to our loved ones, and taking time for ourselves are all important. This sharp division between the various facets of our existence contributes to decreased stress and increased job and personal happiness.

Third, being proactive rather than reactive is made possible by effective time management. If we don't plan, we can discover that most of what we do is a reaction to what is happening in the world. By putting time management techniques into practice, we can take control and focus our efforts on the objectives that truly matter. We can take control of our circumstances this way rather than just reacting to external ones.

Furthermore, time management skills enhance our capacity for decision-making. Our decisions can be hurried and less wise when we are under duress. We can lessen this strain, give ourselves time to think things through and make wise judgments by managing our time.

Finally, effective time management has been linked to improved mental health. Feel as though there is too much and insufficient time to do it. We may prevent work overload and reduce stress by implementing time management techniques, which improves our mental health.

To put it briefly, time management techniques are essential to our daily existence. They enhance our emotional health and sense of fulfillment in life, making us more effective and productive. We can have more satisfying and balanced lives if we embrace and put these strategies into practice.

Establishing SMART Objectives: Goal setting is key to efficient time management. Setting and meeting goals make managing your time effectively, prioritizing your responsibilities, and tracking your progress difficult. Establishing clear, concise objectives gives you focus, inspiration, and a plan for optimizing your time. The SMART goals framework is one of the most well-liked and successful goal-setting strategies.

SMART stands for Time-bound, Specific, Measurable, Achievable, and Relevant.Establishing SMART goals ensures your targets are precise, doable, and time-bound.

Specific: Well-defined objectives eliminate all possibility of confusion. They provide answers to the what, why, and how queries. Rather than aiming for a general objective such as "Improve my time management," a more targeted one could be "Reduce time spent on social media during work hours by 50%."

Measurable: Measurable objectives let you monitor your development and recognize when you've reached them. They offer a definite measure of success and are measurable. The objective in the example above is measurable since it is simple to gauge how much time is spent away from social media.

Achievable goals are reasonable and doable in light of your available resources, abilities, and limitations. Establishing objectives that stretch you but are yet doable is crucial. Unrealistic goals can cause dissatisfaction and demotivation.

Relevant: Relevant Aims are in line with your larger beliefs and aims. They ought to be significant and aid in your accomplishment and general development. Make sure your objectives align with your career and personal goals.

Time-bound: Time-bound objectives have a predetermined end date or duration. This increases the sense of urgency and keeps you from putting things off. Setting and meeting deadlines forces you to accept responsibility for your actions.

SMART goal integration can revolutionize your time management approach. It turns intangible goals into doable strategies. Rather than aiming to "be more productive," for example, you may set a SMART goal such as "Complete all project tasks by the end of the workday, allowing 30 minutes for final review before submission."

SMART goals give tasks structure and clarity, facilitating efficient time management and prioritization. They act as road maps for your time management initiatives, assisting you in maintaining focus on the important things and tracking your development as you go. SMART objectives are an effective tool for transforming your time into a useful and productive resource, whether in your personal or professional life.

Self-Soothing for General Health

Taking care of one's own physical, mental, and emotional health is known as self-care. It entails accepting accountability for one's health and wellbeing and implementing the required adjustments to enhance it. Taking care of oneself involves not just one's physical health but also one's mental and emotional wellness.

There are various categories under which self-care can be classified, such as mental, emotional, and physical self-care. Exercise, a healthy diet, adequate sleep, and abstaining from drugs are all examples of physical self-care. Writing, reading, practicing mindfulness, and meditation are examples of mental self-care. Journaling, counseling, and engaging in self-compassion exercises are examples of emotional self-care.

It's critical to practice physical self-care to preserve general wellbeing. Frequent exercise enhances cardiovascular health and aids in maintaining a healthy weight. Maintaining physical health also requires a balanced diet since it gives the body the nutrition to function correctly. Physical health also benefits from getting enough sleep, enabling the body to mend and regenerate. Maintaining abstinence from dangerous substances like smoke and excessive alcohol intake can also enhance physical wellbeing.

Maintaining mental health and lowering the risk of mental health problems like depression and anxiety need mental self-care. Because reading and writing can enhance cognitive function and lower stress levels, they can be utilized as mental self-care since they can lessen anxiety and increase focus; mindfulness exercises and meditation can also be utilized as a mental self-care.

Maintaining emotional wellbeing and lowering the risk of emotional illnesses like depression and anxiety require emotional self-care. Since journaling enables people to process their feelings and ideas, it can be utilized as an emotional self-care tool. As it enables people to talk to a professional about their feelings and ideas, seeing a therapist can also be utilized as a kind of emotional self-care. Being kind and understanding to oneself is made possible by engaging in self-compassion practices, which can also be utilized as an emotional self-care strategy.

Being aware of one's own physical, mental, and emotional wellbeing is a continuous practice that goes into self-care. It's critical to incorporate self-care into everyday activities and remember to care for oneself even throughout trying circumstances.

Remembering that self-care entails a lifetime commitment to looking after oneself rather than a quick fix is also critical.

Apart from the pursuits above, self-care might encompass activities such as taking outdoor walks, enjoying music, engaging in yoga, or creating a skincare regimen. It's also critical to have a strong social network. Developing and upholding positive relationships with friends and family can be a crucial part of self-care since they give people a feeling of community and emotional support.

Self-care can improve one's physical, mental, and emotional wellbeing and is crucial for general wellbeing. It's critical to incorporate self-care into everyday activities and remember to care for oneself even throughout trying circumstances. Treat yourself with compassion and kindness, and commit to self-care for the rest of your life.

Ava was a young woman who once lived in a tiny village tucked away in the middle of a forest. Nothing pleased Ava more than to assist others; she was a kind and compassionate person. All those who knew her loved and respected her, and she devoted her days to serving the needs of her community.

Ava managed a busy schedule, yet she always found time for herself. She made sure to practice self-care in many ways every day since she felt it was crucial to preserving her own wellbeing. She would take a gentle yoga class in the morning, eat a hearty meal, and then go outside and enjoy the beauty of the surrounding forest.

Ava scheduled time for mental wellness as well. She loved to read and kept a journal, and she discovered that these activities allowed her to decompress and work through her feelings. She also discovered that mindfulness and meditation training enabled her to manage her stress and remain in the present.

For Ava, emotional self-care was as essential. She understood that for her to be able to assist others, she needed to take care of her emotional health. She scheduled time daily to communicate with her family and let them know how she felt. She also discovered that being gentle and understanding with oneself was facilitated by her self-compassion practices.

Ava's self-care regimen became a regular element of her daily schedule. She discovered that she could better look after other people by looking for herself. She became well-known as a ray of hope and light in the village, and her neighbors looked to her for leadership and encouragement.

Handling Diversion
Typical Workplace Diversions

Distractions have a big effect on how well you manage your time. Frequent sources of workplace distractions include social media use, constant email notifications, loud work settings, and lengthy meetings. Effectively managing these distractions begins with acknowledging them.

Techniques for Reducing Distractions

Set work priorities: Prioritize critical chores before lower-priority ones.

✐ Designate certain times for work: Set aside dedicated periods for work.

Employ tools for productivity: During working hours, block distracting websites or apps.

✓ Express boundaries: Inform your coworkers when you require unbroken work time.

You may improve your focus and productivity by implementing these methods and setting up a distraction-free workstation.

The subsequent chapters will cover time management tools and applications, stress management and work-life balance strategies, and effective communication and collaboration techniques.

Chapter 8: Collaboration and Effective Communication

Effective Gatherings

Though they are essential to working life, meetings can be a major time waster if they are not conducted well. Clearly state the goal and agenda to maximize the time in your meeting.

- Only invite those who are truly necessary.
- Establish a rigorous deadline and follow it.

Encourage involvement and steer the conversation in the right direction.

You can cooperate effectively, exchange information, and make effective decisions in meetings.

Email management Managing emails may quickly turn into a time-consuming chore. Effectively manage your inbox by setting aside time to read and reply to emails.

▰ To keep your emails organized, use labels and filters.

▰ Unsubscribe from newsletters that are not needed.

▰ Set email priorities according to deadlines and significance.

By implementing these strategies, you may lessen email-related distractions and ensure that your inbox doesn't become a continual source of interruption.

Recognizing Your Time Management Difficulties

While attempting to improve ourselves, we will unavoidably run into some obstacles. A common excuse for not achieving one's goals is a lack of time. Ironically, people frequently choose not to reflect on their past choices regarding their time. If you follow along, you ought to be clear of this problem. Be mindful while you acknowledge and celebrate this for a time. While there are other challenges you can encounter—some unique to your environment—let's look at some of the more typical difficulties we might encounter while implementing time management.

Overcommitting to multiple tasks is another common issue. We've looked at it so much that it's easy to jot down dozens of things we'd like to do daily. However, there's a serious issue here. Alec Mackenzie correctly identifies a lack of priorities as the cause of this problem in his book The Time Trap. He states, "You are leaving the future to chance if you don't have goals, priorities, and planning."

The most common causes of this are insecurity, perfectionism, and overconfidence. It is strengthened even more by our drive to pursue accomplishments. Fortunately, effective time management includes resolving this problem. Chapter 2 will cover goal-setting and prioritization, and subsequent sections will address effective communication. These abilities will help us avoid becoming victims of this.

Furthermore, a lot of coworkers have had difficulty saying no. Saying that you should turn down certain duties to perform better at work seems paradoxical. However, it's simpler for someone to overwork themselves if they just accept every duty for which they are competent. Furthermore, it snowballs into that unique feature, becoming commonplace and replaceable instead of priceless. I wouldn't advise you to overthrow your employer because they attempted to make too many demands. Instead, take a conciliatory stance towards the issue. Bring up your existing burden and discuss how the additional assignment might hurt the business. Interestingly, there is a solution where everyone on the team works well together.

Even though these two mistakes are frequently made, there are many others that we haven't yet covered. Procrastination and poor communication are two of them that are covered later in the book. However, let's not get ahead of ourselves. I would like you to take a moment to consider your difficulties with time management. Put it in writing and share some strategies for overcoming it.

You'll want to pay extra attention to what you read in this other section of the book. Or this irritated area is extremely particular. Using the structures in this book should, in any case, be quite beneficial. It might only leave a small wrinkle. And it's alright. Curvature can be smoothed out.

Next, consider a few of your time management strong points. Do you excel at creating charts that are simple to understand? Or do you have exceptional data analysis skills? You're great at neatly dividing a project into sections! These and a plethora of other skills will be of use to you. Don't be afraid to use your imagination when coming up with these. My roommate in college had a wonderful kitchen, which helped him have a good start every morning. Just as you did with your challenges, you should record these strengths.

We are often badly impacted by poor time management. First and foremost, it may negatively affect how well we perform at work. It has been demonstrated that improper time and project management frequently results in partial or complete losses, making time for new endeavors more challenging. And although that much is obvious and detrimental to us, the reverse is also true. Let's examine a few more advantages you might experience by maximizing each hour.

Chapter 4: Effective Scheduling and Planning

Plan of action: Set aside time weekly and monthly to focus on your tasks and objectives.

These days, planning and scheduling well is crucial in a world full of distractions and competing demands. This "Efficient Planning and Scheduling" pamphlet will guide you whether you're attempting to meet personal goals, manage a busy household, or succeed professionally. We'll take you on a journey to create a weekly and monthly plan that allows you to take back control of your life and allocate time for your objectives and obligations.

Organizing and Timetables: A Craft

Acknowledge the significance of scheduling and planning for success.

Find out the tangible benefits of effective time management.

Establishing the Foundation

Find the techniques and resources that might support your efforts to schedule and plan.

Choose your own goals and objectives to assist you in scheduling.

The Weekly Timetable You Must Establish

Check out the detailed process for making a weekly schedule.

Take into account a variety of time-blocking methods and approaches for optimal productivity.

The Craft of Monthly Scheduling

Acknowledge the importance of a broad, all-encompassing perspective.

Learn how to align your monthly objectives with your weekly plan.

Your Life in Harmony

Learn what "work-life balance" means and how it affects your schedule.

Discover how to maintain your motivation as you work for your objectives.

Effective Task Management

Find ways to transform your dreams into manageable tasks.

Make the most of your time by prioritizing your tasks effectively.

How to Handle Unexpected Modifications

Prepare yourself for unanticipated events and disruptions, as they are unavoidable.

Make arrangements for modifying your timetable without sacrificing your goals.

Tracking Your Development and Modifying Your Path

Discover how to assess your progress and identify your areas for improvement.

As you gain comprehension, contemplate methods to enhance your schedule.

Psychology of time management

Learn more about time management psychology.

Procrastination tendencies and a need to conquer mental challenges often.

Real-Life Success Stories

Learn from those whose lives have been enhanced by planning and scheduling.

Discover how they overcame challenges to achieve their goals.

Organizing and planning a way of life

Discover how to incorporate schedule and planning into your daily activities.

Learn how to use advanced tactics for more successful time management.

Chapter 2: Calculating Time

Engineers and construction estimators must invest many hours in solving complex mathematical equations to determine how long it will take to complete projects worth billions of dollars. Even though missing deadlines can occasionally cost millions of dollars daily, these projects frequently exceed budget because of calculation errors. How can a business manager ever hope to predict project time if these professionals who are paid to do so frequently come up short?

You must be proficient in time estimation to plan meetings, appointments, assignments, procedures, and projects.

Experience

How long did it take to do this assignment the last time? What has changed from the previous time this project or job was completed? Has technology, manpower, logistics, or process changed?

Citation

To what extent can you gather references? Employee input, product delivery estimates, time estimates from contracted labor, etc.

Dependent Elements

What resources or individuals are needed for this project or task?

Are vendors producing parts that need to be shipped? Are certain project components being outsourced?

Parts

Divide a job into manageable chunks and calculate the approximate time for each.

10 9 8 7 6 Capital 5 Budget 4 3 Cash Flow 2 1 0

View the Unexpected

List all the unanticipated events that can cause your project to be delayed. Make a plan for each person's recovery. Now, calculate the expenses and duration of these scenarios.

Estimating a Project

Budget: What impact will money have on the project?

Will cash flow concerns cause any potential delays in the project?

In what case will capital run out if cash flow is reduced?

By the project's conclusion, the budget should ideally have used all the necessary capital from cash flow and cash on hand.

Give yourself more time for planning as well. As your project progresses, many activities and initiatives require extra planning time for progress reviews. Add the amount of time you anticipate needing for further planning.

Add in the time you'll need to hire any more staff or outsource work.

As many OUT support operations as possible should be moved to secondary time slots.

Your Schedule of Time

Most SME owners keep a careful eye on their finances. They check their bank balance, credit card statements, balance sheets, and profit and loss statements. They calculate cash flow, look for the greatest loan deals, haggle over prices, and create budgets and forecasts. However, very few of these same SME owners manage their time effectively!

Keep a log of your time on each activity and appointment as you move through the day by noting how much time each one truly takes. You can see exactly how you spend your time by tracking your time. Add up all the time you set aside for assignments and activities by the end of the first month. Next, add up the entire time you spent completing these assignments. Take the real time spent and deduct it from the total time given. Your time's profit or loss will be the outcome.

An Overview Of Time Management For Entrepreneurs

Recognizing the Value of Team Management and Delegation

Effectively using one's time is essential to running a successful business. Any establishment's ability to effectively manage and allocate scarce resources can make or break its success. A business owner's wide range of responsibilities includes:

Overseeing day-to-day operations.

Managing funds.

Conducting marketing campaigns.

Making well-informed decisions.

With so many responsibilities to manage, it is critical to organize your time to prioritize specific activities and communicate responsibilities effectively. Delegation among coworkers or subordinates is a useful task management strategy to accomplish this prioritizing.

This section will examine how important it is for entrepreneurs to set aside and manage their time. We will also detail how management and delegating strategies can increase output while helping someone realize their professional goals.

The Significance of Time Management for Entrepreneurs

For an entrepreneur, time is more valuable than almost everything else. One can maximize their limited resources and focus on high-priority projects by managing their time well. As a result, this maximizes the number of hours that can be spent while achieving goals efficiently.

Inadequate scheduling and prioritization can lead to missed deadlines, lower-than-ideal work quality, and decreased productivity. These deficits reduce revenue streams, which has a major impact on your company's financial situation. On the other hand, proficient time management can assist you in:

You must prioritize the most important jobs and give them the attention they require if you want to maximize your productivity.

To improve efficiency, pinpoint places to cut down on time and simplify procedures.

Assign responsibilities to your team members so that you may devote more of your time to making strategic decisions.

Through reducing the causes of stress and fatigue.

The Functions of Teamwork and Delegation in Time Management

For entrepreneurs, efficient control over time is contingent upon the appropriate work allocation. Assigning tasks to your team members allows you to delegate some responsibilities and prioritize more complex projects that require more time and effort. The execution of effective delegation necessitates thoughtful planning and consideration to ensure that tasks are assigned suitably and that they are completed to a high standard.

Team management is also essential to maximize output and accomplish organizational objectives. To help your team reach its full potential, it is your responsibility as an owner to inspire and guide them. This entails laying out precise guidelines, offering encouragement and criticism, and praising and rewarding their achievements.

Concluding

In this chapter, we've covered the value of time management for business owners and the part teamwork and delegation play in increasing output and accomplishing objectives. You can free yourself from time restraints by allocating work to team members and efficiently prioritizing your daily activities. This will enable a sharper focus on strategic decision-making, which will increase output production efficiency and profit margins at the same time.

Practice: Determine Which Tasks to Assign

One of the most important aspects of efficient time management is task delegation. Business owners must determine which jobs can be assigned to team members. By assigning responsibilities effectively, you can free up more time to concentrate on important business-related activities.

- Create a list of all the tasks you perform daily for your company.
- Evaluate each task to determine whether you are the only person who can complete it or if another team member can handle it.
- Decide which team member is most suited to do each task with a delegable option.
- Call a meeting to discuss the task and establish clear guidelines and expectations for that team member.

- Keep an eye on how the task at hand is doing and provide aid and feedback as required.

You may boost productivity overall and allow more time to concentrate on important business tasks by effectively delegating work.

The Basics of Individual Growth

Describe personal growth.

Personal growth is known as becoming a better version of oneself in one's job, relationships, health, and general well-being. It includes a path devoted to realizing and pursuing one's potential.

For those with intelligence, why is it valuable?

Knowledge is a thirst that intelligent people have, and they can efficiently satisfy this thirst with personal development. It allows people to grow, overcome obstacles, and achieve their goals.

The Advantages of Personal Growth: growth has benefits such as improved self-awareness, increased confidence, sharpened problem-solving skills, increased productivity, strengthened interpersonal relationships, and improved physical and mental health.

How to Begin Your Personal Development Journey:

There are various methods to start your journey toward improvement. Think about the following recommendations:

● Set objectives: Begin by determining your life's ambitions. You may plan to accomplish your goals after you clearly grasp them.

Determine your advantages and disadvantages; Consider your strengths and opportunities for development. Knowing your strengths and areas for improvement allows you to concentrate on improving those areas.

- Look for someone who has already accomplished your goals to serve as a mentor or coach. They can offer assistance and direction as you progress through your growth. Participate in workshops or courses; some resources provide chances to learn new skills and promote personal development.
- Read books and articles; delve into development-related material, which might offer insightful information.
- Act: Ultimately, the most important stage is to take action toward your objectives—making a start is essential.

In summary, having a happy and meaningful life is a function of personal development. It's critical to remember that progress is a continuous process rather than a destination, although paved with ups and downs.

Those who are intelligent frequently have an understanding of their talents and shortcomings. However, they could find it difficult to build on their areas of weakness or leverage their strengths. Overcoming these obstacles can involve personal development and progress.

In addition, intelligent people could be driven to achieve. They might not know how to define objectives or build a thorough strategy. Development activities might provide direction in this area.

Furthermore, it's not unusual for intellectual people to hang around with other intelligent people. However, they can discover that they are not surrounded by people who can push them intellectually or help them along their path of personal development.

Chapter Ten: Time Difference

Error #1: Setting priorities

The most frequent time management grievances I hear involve creating priorities at work. They may be divided into two categories:

the employee struggles to balance several tasks and cannot establish their priorities, or the supervisor struggles to determine the employee's priorities. The employer frequently identifies every project as equally vital, leading employees to give up in frustration and merely guess which project to focus on. If they guess incorrectly or the boss is unreasonable, this could lead to drama and tension later. Whether the worker or the supervisor fails to set priorities, a scrambling employee may easily get overwhelmed and overworked (which is another classic time trap; see below). Although it sounds simple, the answer could be challenging to implement: politely request that your supervisor set project priorities. Next, carefully prioritize your to-do list and the things that need to be done. Give each other priority based on their relative worth.

Distractions and Interruptions

This time waster is anything habitual but not scheduled that interferes with someone's concentration and reduces their output at work. Meetings and crises are separate categories and do not count. I bet you could list the numerous distractions and interruptions that affect your productivity at work, like ringing phones, noisy neighbors, micromanaging supervisors, and coworkers who drop in at strange times to fill up a whole page (or more). Almost one-third of the complaints in this category are related to communication problems, which are a constant source of trouble for all of us, particularly regarding email and phone calls. This specific trap calls for a strict application of self-control to escape. If you become sidetracked or interrupted, take the appropriate precautions to avoid it. Have your executive assistant secure entry for you if you have one. If not, sharpen your attention. To drown out noise, turn on music or ambient sounds. Close your browser and disable email alerts. When you don't have time to answer calls, send them to voicemail and check your voicemail sometimes. Take a little break and work from home one day a week, or go somewhere quieter.

Trap #3: Excessive labor or stress

"There's not enough time in the day to do everything!" is the main issue. Within the harsh confines of a 24-hour workday, workers can only exert so much energy, given the human need for relaxation (and sanity). Nobody can extend or bargain with time as a limitation. Establish strict time management by eliminating pointless activities from your calendar and focusing intently and relentlessly.

Look at each task and see if you've been performing too much of it—that is, can your downstream user get by with less work? Assign the assignment to the appropriate person if it truly belongs to them. Seek opportunities to assign work to others as often as possible and engage in deliberate abandonment. If you run out of time for anything that isn't very important, let it go. Consider your to-do list a "want to do" rather than a "must do" list. When combined, these actions are significant and can assist you in addressing the overwhelming beast before it consumes you. However, they just mark the start of a legitimate prioritization effort.

Trap #4: Insufficient Self-Control

Some people find that their largest issue with time management is simply a lack of self-discipline or the inability to muster the courage to refuse distractions or to persevere through tasks until they are completed. But a lot of people won't acknowledge it. Many workers struggle to focus or try to multitask excessively. They juggle too many projects at once, which also reflects planning and prioritization problems. Some struggle with goal-setting or maintaining focus, while some simply cannot complete tasks on schedule. To overcome these obstacles, resolve to focus on a task through to completion, firm up your resolve, and crack the whip on yourself. Of those who struggle with self-discipline, about 25% believe that procrastination is more serious than just a lack of concentration. Usually, they are intimidated by large, intricate undertakings. Therefore, in addition to giving the issue your full attention, divide it into manageable portions. Establish goals, take a deep breath, and go to work.

Trap #5: A lack of structure

Many employees accept a high degree of turmoil in their lives, which causes them to become mired in a state of disorganization over time. Data is frequently misplaced or lost. These employees occasionally become overwhelmed by managing the boss (or subordinates), organizing, filing, tracking action items, and overseeing the entire project because they lack a systematic method for processing information. Develop a rational, uncomplicated organizing system, make the most of your email program, and handle all the information that comes into your life. Never let stuff accumulate, and never hesitate to act upon each piece of information that comes across your desk, be it a voicemail, an email, or a piece of paper. Always allot time for preparation. From time to time, take a step back and assess the big picture to ensure everything operates as it should. When required, address ineffective practices and watch for methods to increase productivity.

6. Scheduling is a trap

Do you find it difficult to complete tasks in your available time? Frequently voiced grievances involve the incapacity to accurately project the duration of particular jobs (a capability acquired through practice) and determining the optimal location for each work on one's schedule. The second scenario necessitates the careful (and strict) application of task prioritizing and triage and the ability to decline new assignments when it is practical. In particular, you need to learn how to let go of things. Your calendar is overflowing with pointless meetings, preventing you from completing critical tasks. Most of us prioritize the simple, enjoyable chores first—at best, an ineffective mindset. Rather, prioritize the difficult, important tasks first. Should time run out, you can let go of the remaining.

Trap#7: Issues with People

The adage "Hell is other people" was attributed to Jean-Paul Sartre, and working with your coworkers can provide several challenges to completing your tasks. Many distractions at work come from other people, as I've already covered. Who hasn't been irritated by coworkers playing loud music or talking in the hallway? The largest time constraints for upper-echelon employees are frequently found in managerial responsibilities, although those are requirements of the position. It is more detrimental to productivity at work when individuals serve as obstacles and bottlenecks. Some appear to do it deliberately, frequently out of pure cussedness. Some don't give a damn about your deadlines. Thus they don't send you crucial information on time. Some people simply never seem to arrive on time, wasting your time.

Additionally, you might have to wait patiently for your supervisor to decide if they are incapable or unwilling to make a choice. There are certain obstacles you can avoid. Some you can break by asking the person blocking you directly what the hold-up is or by intervening to help. In any case, try to clear the path so the workflow can resume. If not, realize that you can do nothing about it and move on to something else.

Trap #8: Emergency Situations

According to my informal study, people's difficulties and the time trap of the unexpected are tied for first place. Human conduct plays a role in most workplace situations in one way or another. Human bottlenecks hog resources, bosses throw urgent tasks at you out of the blue, sluggish coworkers drag their heels till you can hardly meet deadlines, and everything comes due at the last minute. Everyone has been there, and everyone will undoubtedly return. When other people cause a problem, all you can do is react, which means you have to be adaptable at all times. Create procedures and protocols in preparation and instructions for every imaginable kind of emergency to deal with the unexpected when it rears its ugly head. Practice SLLR (Stop, Look, Listen, and Respond) in times of crisis. Once you've gained control over the situation, take immediate action. Your to-do list might need to be reorganized, including moving some items up or down. Allow the extra time you've previously allocated to your schedule to compensate for any gaps. While letting go of as many of your regular chores as possible, do everything you can to handle the new work; while doing so, seek all the assistance you can.

Trap #9: Balancing Work and Life

With everything your organization throws at you, it can occasionally appear like they don't want you to have a life outside of work. Employees often accept excessive hours as background noise. Most people merely want a private life to allow them to go to school, exercise, pursue hobbies, rest and relax, or—the most popular answer—spend more time with their families. Once more, the key to the solution is to maintain a rigorous schedule of self-discipline, brutal task prioritizing, and unwavering scheduling to carve out enough time in your schedule to enjoy life away from work. Try to be as productive and efficient as possible at work so that you may get the most done in the least amount of time, leave the workplace earlier (can you work 10 hours instead of 12?), and have a life.

Trap #10: Gatherings

Face time is essential for every firm to operate. Therefore, meetings will always take up some time in the typical worker's day. They become out of control in certain firms, negatively impacting worker productivity. Finding enough time to complete your work can be challenging when you frequently spend half of the day in back-to-back meetings. Before you accuse me of hyperbole, I know individuals who have held similar positions. Again, unaware individuals are usually the source of poorly run meetings. They make mistakes by wasting other people's time when they ramble on, refuse to get to the point, or just can't communicate effectively. In addition to battling this inclination within yourself, you can escape the meeting trap by reducing the number of meetings you attend, attending only those you genuinely need to, and establishing time limitations that notify everyone of as soon as you get there. After contributing, try to get out of there. Please excuse yourself respectfully and say you have another meeting to attend if the meeting continues longer than planned.

Chapter 6: Workloads and Low-Priority Assignments

Have you ever discovered that you could spend hours on unimportant tasks? Maybe you've worked on low-priority projects or busy work all day, only to find that you haven't advanced your most crucial assignments at the end of the day. Then you are not by yourself.

We frequently find ourselves overloaded with duties and to-do lists in today's environment, which can be stressful. It's simple to get bogged down in the minutiae and concentrate on unimportant things while ignoring the ones that will advance our objectives. For this reason, it's critical to understand the distinction between busy work and high-priority jobs and to develop good time management skills.

Recognizing the issue of busywork is the first step in solving it. Examine your to-do list carefully and decide which items are important and which are not. Are there any items on your list that you might assign to a different person or remove? Are there any jobs you're performing more out of habit or ease of familiarity than out of necessity?

It's time to order your high-priority jobs once you've determined which ones are the busiest. What are the most crucial activities to accomplish to reach your long-term objectives? Which assignments will most affect your professional, personal, or business life? These are the things you ought to be concentrating on. It's crucial to remember that not all projects with the highest priority are the most urgent. Our most important work might frequently be neglected in favor of urgent chores. Because of this, it's critical to develop good prioritization skills to concentrate on the activities that will have the greatest influence on your life.

Using the Eisenhower Matrix is one method of setting a priority list for your high-priority projects. This easy-to-use tool will assist you in differentiating between critical and urgent jobs so that you can efficiently set priorities. There are four quadrants in the matrix:

Important and Urgent: Completing these chores immediately is necessary because they are both important and urgent.

Not urgent yet essential: Although these duties are essential, they are not urgent. They must be planned and completed as quickly as feasible.

Not Important but Urgent: These are not important but urgent jobs. They can frequently be removed or assigned.

Not Important or Urgent: These chores are not urgent or important. They ought to be removed. You can focus on the things that will most impact your life by utilizing the Eisenhower Matrix to prioritize your duties. You can also delegate or eliminate chores that are not important.

Another strategy to deal with the issue of busy work is to create a routine and obvious timetable. High-priority jobs should have designated periods of the day or week, and you should try your best to adhere to this timetable. Doing this lets you block off distractions and concentrate on your most crucial tasks.

In conclusion, low-priority jobs and busy work schedules can be a significant time waster that keeps us from reaching our objectives and leading satisfying lives. We may take charge of our time and invest in our futures by recognizing our hectic job activities, ranking our high-priority chores, and creating explicit timetables and routines. Recall that time is money and that each minute lost is one that we cannot get back.

Accepting Change

"Changing one's attitude is the greatest discovery of all time because it can change one's destiny." —Oprah Winfrey.

Consider the topic of arithmetic, which is dreaded by many. People frequently assume it's challenging and get pessimistic about it. On the other hand, people discover they can succeed when they adopt an optimistic outlook and approach arithmetic. The most important lesson is that unless you make a change, nothing will change.

If you adopt a different perspective, working remotely can become less of a drastic choice and more of an opportunity to obtain multiple rewards. Deciding whether to hire remote workers for your business, yourself, and your staff will get easier.

We all need to have an open and flexible mentality to handle the frequent changes that impact our lives favorably and negatively.

The Requirement for Modification

You must first understand why you must view the unavoidable changes positively if you want to cultivate a mindset that supports change.

Managing Change Right Now

Understanding the idea of remote work, its benefits and drawbacks, and its potential effects on your business and staff is essential to being change-ready. Being knowledgeable can help you deal with any problems that might come up (Everything You Need to Know about the Changing World of Work, per the Economist, 2016).

Accepting Differences

Employers may access a wider range of talent through remote work, which promotes diversity in the workforce and the way they think. We must adjust and learn how to deal with these shifts as the world evolves.

Utilizing Technology In today's world, Technology is a need. In the past, there was widespread concern that employment might be lost due to technological improvements. Rather, Technology has brought about chances for development and advancement.

Imagine a revolutionary device that replaces a manual task with automation. Because of this Technology, workers must acquire new skills to operate, maintain, and guarantee the quality of output rather than lose their jobs. Technology has shown itself to be more of a benefit than a danger.

The Increase in Work from Home

Although remote work has been around for a while, the COVID-19 outbreak helped to popularize it. We discovered that many duties could be completed from home and that we weren't always required to be there.

Before the pandemic, workers in creative professions like writing, design, and art had remote jobs. We all have some experience with its efficacy, so it's time to acknowledge and seize its potential.

The Great Resignation: Juggling Remote Work with Employee Needs

The Great Resignation has brought attention to the necessity of attending to the demands of employees, as individuals are more concerned than ever with their job satisfaction, work-life balance, and general well-being. Companies need to modify their approaches to attract and retain people in the wake of the COVID-19 pandemic by providing flexible work schedules and perks that accommodate a range of preferences.

For example, many workers learned the benefits of working remotely during the pandemic, including the ease of avoiding long commutes, the freedom to better manage their time, and the opportunity to achieve a better work-life balance. Employees, however, quit and looked for jobs that would offer the required perks when some employers failed to comply with their wishes.

Take Audrey's story, a marketing expert who had worked for her employer for five years. She switched to working remotely after the epidemic struck and fell in love with its flexibility.

Audrey discovered that working remotely allowed her to be more productive, spend more time with her family, and have a comfortable workspace. Nevertheless, Audrey's requests to continue working remotely were turned down when her employer switched back to in-person meetings. She quit and looked for work elsewhere when she realized she would lose the equilibrium she had discovered.

Audrey's experience during the Great Resignation was not unusual; it is representative of the experiences of many professionals. Firms must reevaluate their approaches to keep valuable personnel and consider providing remote work options, hybrid schedules, or other flexible solutions. Businesses that adapt to these developments can strengthen their teams, lower employee attrition, and maintain their competitiveness in the dynamic labor market.

Furthermore, the global integration trend—where companies cooperate with specialists worldwide—has been accelerated by the increase in remote work. Due to reduced geographical and time zone constraints, businesses can now access a large talent pool. Thanks to the globalization of the workforce, people are now more empowered to look for jobs that fit their values and tastes without being limited by geography.

For instance, Rajnish, an Indian software developer, successfully landed a remote job with a US-based IT company. With this chance, he could pursue his passion for work in an area he was enthusiastic about and still benefits from working remotely, which included taking care of his aging parents and striking a healthy work-life balance. John's narrative demonstrates how international integration can foster ties advantageous to businesses and employees.

Due to The Great Resignation, employees are looking for organizations that fit their needs. Global integration, flexible scheduling, and remote work are essential for businesses to retain top personnel. These elements foster a valued and empowered workforce and increase employee happiness.

The business and its employees succeed and thrive when these elements are implemented. To build a resilient and flexible future in the post-pandemic world, businesses must comprehend and adjust to the shifting terrain of employee preferences.

Chapter 3: How Can Time Management and Productivity Be Improved? What Are the Proven Principles and Strategies?

This chapter will cover some of the most popular and successful ideas and techniques for enhancing your productivity and time management abilities.

● Examples and case studies of how these strategies and concepts have benefited successful individuals or organizations. ● How to apply these principles and methods to other aspects of your life, such as work, study, home, health, hobbies, etc.

What are the tried-and-true methods for increasing productivity and time management?

A variety of ideas and techniques can enhance your productivity and time management. Not all of them might be appropriate for you or your circumstances. As a result, you must experiment to see what suits you the best.

The following are a few of the most popular and successful ideas and techniques you can try:

Assigning SMART objectives: Specific, Measurable, Achievable, Relevant (Realistic), and Time-bound is what SMART stands for. These standards provide your objectives definition, realism, and tracking. Establishing SMART goals will assist you in keeping your attention on your objectives, plan of action, and deadline. It can also assist you in dividing your objectives into more doable chunks.

● Setting task priorities: Setting priorities for your work involves selecting the most crucial or urgent things to complete. Setting priorities for your job will help you make better use of your time, reduce wasted time on pointless or unimportant tasks, and lessen the stress of workloads and deadlines. Numerous ways to prioritize work include the ABCD analysis, the Priority Matrix, or the Eisenhower Method.

● Planning ahead: Planning involves planning for your duties or goals. Planning can help you organize your time better, identify potential challenges or possibilities, and avoid procrastination or last-minute rush. There are numerous tools for preparing ahead, such as calendars, schedules, action plans, checklists, etc.

● Delegating and outsourcing: Delegating and outsourcing involve assigning some of your work or obligations to others who can accomplish them better or faster than you. Delegating and outsourcing can help you save time, energy, and resources, focus on your key strengths or objectives, and harness the skills or knowledge of others. There are numerous ways to delegate or outsource jobs, such as hiring freelancers, contractors, or agencies, using internet platforms or services, or asking for help from colleagues, family, or friends.

● Batching and automating: Batching and automating entail putting similar or repetitive tasks together and completing them simultaneously or with minimal intervention. Batching and automating can help eliminate interruptions, diversions, or switching costs, boost efficiency, consistency, or quality, and free up time for more creative or strategic work. There are numerous ways to batch or automate processes, such as employing apps, software, or tools, developing templates, scripts, or workflows, or setting up rules, alerts, or reminders.

● Eliminating distractions: Eliminating distractions implies removing anything that diverts your attention or interest away from your tasks. Eliminating distractions can help you boost your focus, motivation, or quality of work, reduce errors, blunders, or rework, and attain a flow or optimal performance. There are numerous techniques to reduce distractions, such as turning off notifications, texts, or calls, closing superfluous tabs, windows, or apps, using headphones, earplugs, or noise-canceling devices, decluttering your desk, workspace, or environment, or creating boundaries with others.

Instruments For Assessment And Modification

Digital instruments for evaluating progress

Digital technologies are now necessary to assess time management progress. Evaluate our daily patterns and identify development opportunities. Numerous platforms and applications are available to assist us in this regard.

With time monitoring tools like Toggl is Hours, users can precisely log the amount of time they spend on each work, giving them a clear picture of how their time is being spent. Additionally, these systems can produce reports that aid in identifying patterns, such as times of distraction or periods of peak production.

Similarly, work managers facilitating work organization and prioritization provide a thorough overview of ongoing projects and tasks via Asana or Trello. Its progress tracking features also let you monitor how a job or project is coming along, spot delays, and modify the timeline as needed.

Time management tools like Google Calendar and Microsoft Outlook are also beneficial companions. They let you arrange meetings, set reminders, and plan activities, making it easier to remember obligations and due dates.

Relaxing and practicing meditation might be crucial for effective time management. Apps for wellness like Calm or Headspace assist in stress management and enhance focus, which is essential for efficient time management.

Additionally, other programs integrate multiple of these features. RescueTime and Timely Alone can track the time spent on various tasks and offer productivity insights, goal-setting capabilities, and tailored suggestions to enhance time management.

It's crucial to discuss online learning platforms in addition to apps. Enrolling in time management courses and training on Coursera, LinkedIn Learning, or Udemy platforms.

Smartwatches and other wearable technology can be helpful as well. These gadgets can monitor our everyday activities and provide information on stress levels, physical activity, and sleep patterns, which can impact how well we manage our time.

Everybody works differently and has different demands. Consequently, it's critical to experiment with many tools and select the ones that best fit our requirements and way of life.

Furthermore, even while these tools can be quite beneficial, avoiding becoming overly reliant on them is crucial. Core components of efficient time management remain self-control and dedication to our objectives.

Finally, remember that this approach involves more than just these instruments. It is necessary to regularly and consciously reflect on our habits and behaviors to assess our development. We won't be able to identify areas for development and modify our time management techniques until after this investigation.

Nowadays, digital instruments for progress assessment are indispensable. They provide us with a wealth of tools that let us precisely monitor our actions, examine our patterns, and modify our tactics to manage our time more effectively. But its application needs to be balanced by a dedication to our objectives on a personal level and ongoing introspection about our choices. We can only sustain and enhance our time management in this way.

Chapter 4: Leveraging the Power of Attention and Focus to Increase Productivity and

Efficiency Enhancing focus and concentration on the activity at hand is crucial to raising productivity. To lessen interruptions, set up a specific workplace, turn off notifications, and shut down any unnecessary tabs or programs on your computer. Engage in deep work, which spends much uninterrupted time concentrating on one task. Use techniques like time blocking to designate specific time slots for focused work. Focus and concentration help you do tasks more swiftly and efficiently.

Employing time-blocking strategies like the Commodore Technique The Commodore Technique is a well-known time management strategy that advocates working in short bursts and taking short pauses in between. Set a timer for a specific amount of time, usually twenty-five minutes (called a "Pomodoro"), and focus solely on the task at hand for that duration. After every Commodore, take a little nap, and then after a few Pomodoros, take a longer one.

This approach reduces burnout, increases productivity, and helps with focus. Try experimenting with other time-blocking strategies that work for you, such as the 52-17 ratio or the 90-minute work period. Try out a few different approaches until you identify the one that works best for your workflow.

Utilizing technology to assign and automate

Thanks to technology, many tools and resources are now available, which can boost output and efficiency. Look for opportunities to automate repetitive tasks with software or apps. Use productivity tools and apps to organize your tasks, collaborate with colleagues, and organize your duties. Assign tasks to others that they can complete to free up your time so you may focus on more crucial responsibilities. Project management tools, communication channels, and cloud storage are used to enhance collaboration and ensure smooth information sharing. Using technology effectively can speed up procedures, increase output, and save time.

Effective multitasking as opposed to single-tasking for productivity: While multitasking is often associated with increased productivity, it has the opposite effect. Research indicates that multitasking requires split attention, reducing productivity and increasing errors. Instead, focus on single-tasking, committing all your attention to one task at a time. Prioritize your tasks and accomplish them in that order, devoting all your focus and energy to each before going on to the next. Focusing on one work at a time will enable you to complete it more quickly and with better results.

Techniques that boost productivity and efficiency must be used for effective time management. By applying time-blocking strategies such as the Pomodoro Technique, focusing and paying attention, and employing technology for

1.4 The ABCDE Prioritisation Method

Another prioritization strategy that can help you focus on the most crucial things and efficiently manage your time is the ABCDE approach. Using this system, you designate a letter (A, B, C, D, or E) to every task on your to-do list according to how urgent and important it is. The ABCDE approach can be applied as follows:

1. A-Tasks: These are the most crucial assignments, failing which could have dire repercussions. They should come on your list of priorities and be finished first. Examples include completing projects with a high priority, fulfilling deadlines, and attending to pressing problems.

2. B-Tasks: These assignments are crucial, but failing to finish them right away will not have as serious of an impact. They ought to be

finished following A-tasks. A few examples are attending meetings, replying to non-urgent emails, and working on projects with future deadlines.

3. C-Tasks: After A and B tasks are finished, these chores—which are neither urgent nor significant—can be finished. Even though they don't have any immediate implications if they are not completed, these chores could increase your total productivity. Routine administrative work, personal errands, and unnecessary meetings are a few examples.

4. D-Tasks: You can assign these jobs to others to free up your time so you can concentrate on other crucial duties. Tasks that are monotonous, outside of your area of expertise, or that someone else could perform more quickly are a few examples.

5. Electronic tasks: You should eliminate these since they don't help you reach your objectives or be more productive overall. Some examples

are time-wasting hobbies, excessive social media use, and pointless commitments.

Examine your to-do list and give each activity a letter according to its urgency and importance to implement the ABCDE approach. Prioritize finishing A-tasks, B-tasks, and C-tasks in order of importance. To make more time for higher-priority work, assign D-tasks whenever possible and eliminate E-tasks.

You may efficiently prioritize your duties and make sure that you devote your time and effort to the important things by employing the ABCDE approach.

Chapter 5: Balancing Work and Life

We'll talk about the value of work-life balance in this chapter and offer advice on successfully managing your time to reach this objective.

1. The value of work-life balance: We risk burnout, stress, and lower productivity when we put work before other aspects of our lives. It's critical to understand that our lives consist of many facets, including our families, hobbies, and self-care, which are just as significant as our jobs. We may raise our productivity at work and improve our general wellbeing by striking a healthy work-life balance.

2. Set priorities: Managing your time efficiently is critical to attaining a work-life balance. Decide which chores are most important and plan them for when you are most productive. Recognize how much you can do in a day, and try not to take on more than you can do.

3. Establish boundaries: Achieving a work-life balance requires establishing boundaries. Pay

attention to work-related chores while at work; don't check your emails or answer business calls while on vacation. Prioritize your family, interests, and self-care routines at home. Establish clear boundaries between business and home life if you work from home by designating a specific workplace and time slot.

4. Take care of yourself: Keeping a work-life balance requires self-care. Schedule time for enjoyable, calming pursuits like reading, exercising, and meditation. Eat a balanced diet, get adequate sleep, and take breaks during the day to rejuvenate. If you take care of yourself, you'll have more energy and focus to handle your work and enjoy your personal life.

5. Seek assistance: Finding a work-life balance can be difficult, but assistance makes it simpler. Seek assistance from friends, family, and coworkers, and don't hesitate to ask for

assistance when needed. If you're feeling stressed or burned out, consider signing up for a support group or getting help from a professional.

You can attain a healthy work-life balance and enhance your general well-being by prioritizing time, establishing boundaries, engaging in self-care, and asking for help.

In the next part, we'll talk about multitasking and whether it's a useful productivity strategy.

Explore The Psychological Underpinnings Of Why Humans Procrastinate

Many people have been fascinated and perplexed by the procrastination riddle throughout history. We must explore the psychological underpinnings of this intriguing phenomenon to fully understand its complexity. The psychological motivators beyond the surface causes of procrastination can shed light on the intricate relationships, behaviors, and motivations within our minds. This chapter deconstructs a complicated picture of human conduct by examining the psychological elements underlying our tendency to put things off.

Fear of not succeeding and self-doubt

Often, the dread of failing lies at the core of procrastination. The mere fear of falling short of one's or other people's expectations might set off a psychological response that makes people put off doing a task entirely. It's possible for the dread of failing to become so intense that it seems simpler to put off a task indefinitely rather than face the possible frustration of falling short of perfection. Alongside the dread of failing, self-doubt contributes to procrastination. Procrastination on jobs requiring effort or ability is more common among those with self-doubt or mistrust of their abilities. The overwhelming barrier of the subconscious thought that they would be unable to handle the issue keeps people in the procrastination loop.

Poor self-confidence

The term "self-efficacy," first used by psychologist Albert Bandura, describes a person's confidence to finish activities or produce desired outcomes. Procrastination is more common in those with poor self-efficacy because they believe their efforts are in vain and their abilities are insufficient. A self-fulfilling prophecy may result from this lack of confidence, whereby their delay confirms their perception of their incompetence. Fascinatingly, self-efficacy can vary by region. People may procrastinate in some parts of their lives because they feel unqualified, yet they may feel competent in other areas. Procrastination can be fought by strengthening one's self-efficacy via mastery experiences and encouraging feedback.

Trend of Instant Gratification

The allure of rapid gratification greatly influences human behavior. Our evolutionary past, in which survival has depended on collecting resources rapidly, is the cause of this instant reward bias. This propensity can cause us to put short-term gratification ahead of long-term objectives in the modern environment. Tasks that promise rewards later compete with instant gratification activities like scrolling through social media, viewing movies, or indulging in comfort food. An inclination for fast gratification is reinforced by the brain's pleasure centers, which react more strongly to rewards immediately. Because of this, it may be challenging for us to focus and exert the necessary effort on things with broad advantages, which eventually causes us to put them off.

Discounting Time and Trends

Time discounting is a cognitive phenomenon where benefits that occur later in life are given less weight. We tend to choose the present over the future due to this bias, which makes it challenging to work on projects that will only be worthwhile after a substantial time and effort commitment. This cognitive distortion is closely linked to the present bias phenomenon, favoring immediate gratification over long-term advantages. Procrastination arises from a contradiction between our current orientation and the needs of tasks that require delayed gratification. We find it difficult to weigh the possible benefits of a quest's future benefits against the difficulty of embarking on it now, so we choose temporary comfort over long-term benefits.

The Effect of Zeigarnik

According to a psychological theory known as the Zeigarnik effect, we tend to recall interrupted or incomplete tasks more vividly than finished ones. This phenomenon puts mental strain on us, bringing the unfinished business of finding closure back to our attention. The Zeigarnik effect can encourage someone to finish a task, but if postponed repeatedly, it can cause procrastination. Ironically, the mental weight of unfinished business accumulates as duties are postponed, leading to tension and anxiety. This pain can eventually become too much, which drives us to finish chores to relieve our mental tension.

4. The Tortoise and the Hare

We are all familiar with this ancient story from Aesop's Fables. The Perry Index number for this piece is 226. It has always been cited as an uplifting tale and can be found in most children's textbooks worldwide in various languages.

A quick hare once took great pride in his running prowess. He used to laugh at the tortoise's slow pace as well. One day, the tortoise, fed up with the hare's constant taunting and worn out from hearing it brag about, decided to challenge it to a race. The news set the jungle ablaze with excitement.

On the day of the race, every animal turned out to witness the show. Like an arrow, the hare shot off down the road and continued running until stopping at a bend. It glanced back and barely saw the tortoise was still close to the starting point. Exclaimed the hare.

The hare then decided to stretch down next to the road and thought, "Let me relax, there's plenty of time."

In the meantime, the turtle continued to move slowly and steadily. Until it crossed the sleeping hare and arrived at the finish line, it never once paused.

The waiting animals let out a loud cheer as they noticed that the tortoise was the first to approach. That noise awakened the hare. It yawned and stretched, horrified to see the tortoise approaching the finish line. It started running as quickly as before, but it was too late. The tortoise had crossed the boundary.

Layman Lessons a. Face disagreements head-on and never back down from them.

In this tale, the tortoise showed no fear in the face of the hare's confrontation. After ignoring the hare's prodding several times, the tortoise gave up and conversed with the animal. We too frequently make compromises in life to keep things amicable. We don't want to harm others, even sacrificing our self-worth. I want to emphasize that we shouldn't be afraid of confrontation rather than suggesting that we should argue with everyone about every little thing.

Life will inevitably bring up conflicts; they cannot be completely avoided. Someone is a chronic people-pleaser if they avoid conflict excessively. They will be losing out on a lot in life. You might avoid short-term confrontations as a people-pleaser who tries to be kind to everyone, but life becomes harder and harder every day. Even goodness needs to have a threshold limit. The Mahabharata, Pandavas, and Shri Krishna try to prevent violence, but conflict is unavoidable once one side violates all lines. Instead of hoping for a life free from conflict or praying for it, let's arm ourselves with the strength to handle disagreements head-on. This little conflict curve illustrates the various stages of conflict, whether a domestic dispute or a war.

When a dispute is just starting, we should try to defuse it. If things get out of hand, we should face the dispute head-on and work through it.

This brings up the subject of self-esteem, which is defined as one's ideas, beliefs, and sentiments about oneself. While some of us have relatively robust and stable self-esteem, others have more brittle self-esteem. You won't be disappointed by unfavorable comments if you know that you are capable of more than you think. You will also not require external reinforcement and praise.

The hare's character demonstrates a weak sense of self-worth, whereas the tortoise's demonstrates a robust one. While the hare boasted about its ability to require outside validation, the turtle knows its capabilities and limitations well.

"Secured self-esteem allows for more exploration by making challenges and the possibility of failure much less daunting, whereas fragile self-esteem leads one to make decisions that protect one's sense of self." People with low self-esteem may be afraid to take risks or do new things for fear of failing, which limits their social, professional, and educational prospects. While pursuing a job, these tendencies might eventually result in indecision and insecurity; in contrast, solid self-esteem is linked to a clearer career path and higher levels of self-efficacy in reaching goals.[8]

The rather confident turtle prepared for a race against a formidable opponent. It was aware it would lose, but it wouldn't be bothered to hear what other creatures had to say. However, the hare burned and humiliated itself instead of defeating the tortoise by a wide margin.

Step 6: The Influence of Stacking Habits

Habit stacking is an effective method for forming and maintaining new behaviors. Connecting a new habit to an existing one can make it easier to incorporate into your daily routine. For instance, add ten minutes if you plan to get ready right after your typical morning routine.

Habit stacking is another option to overcome tardy tendencies. You can help yourself get out the door on time by establishing a new habit. You may also set an alarm for 15 minutes earlier to remind you to keep on schedule if you frequently run late in the afternoon. These prompts have the potential to be quite effective in both forming new habits and ending unhealthy ones.

You may also utilize habit stacking to establish daily routines that remind you of your priorities and ambitions. To help you stay on track throughout the day, consider creating a morning ritual to evaluate your daily agenda and make a goal. Similarly, making it a nightly practice to evaluate your day and record any lessons you learned is a fantastic method to hold yourself responsible.

Maintaining these routines regularly can help you make better decisions and bring about long-lasting change. Thus, don't delay; begin habit stacking right now! A little bit goes a long way when kicking bad tardiness habits and moving closer to your objectives.

Chapter 5: Get Rid of That Distraction! (Beating Time Blindness to Win)

Everyone moves towards the future at sixty minutes every hour, no matter what he does or who he is. –Lincoln S.

Have you ever been engrossed in a task or activity that seems to take on a life of its own or lost track of time? Even though you may begin with the best intentions, hours might quickly pass, and you'll wonder where the time went. If this sounds like you, you might have trouble with distractions and time blindness, which are common issues for those with ADHD.

Consider time blindness as a slippery fish that always evades your grip. It eludes you when you believe you have a firm grasp on it, leaving you bewildered and frustrated. This can be very annoying when you have critical deadlines or jobs to perform. However, you may learn to hang onto that "slippery fish" and improve how you manage your time by employing the appropriate tactics.

Understanding what time blindness is and how it affects you is one of the first steps towards treating it. You can begin to lessen the effects of time blindness by identifying its symptoms, which include underestimating how long tasks will take or losing track of time while working.

The effects of time blindness on productivity will be covered in this chapter. You'll discover more about it, how it impacts those who have ADHD, and how to identify it in yourself. We'll look at various methods for organizing it and setting priorities so you can make the most of your time. We'll also go over how to get past procrastination and perfectionism, two frequent challenges for those with ADHD. We'll look at the underlying reasons for these issues and offer helpful solutions.

Even when everything around you tries to drag you away, a variety of strategies can help you stay focused and control distractions. We can help you with anything from using the power of visualization to dividing work into manageable chunks.

By the time this chapter ends, you'll have a toolkit full of useful techniques to help you eliminate distractions and sharpen your time-management abilities to maximize your productivity and reach your objectives. You'll discover useful techniques for overcoming these obstacles and maintaining accountability. You'll be unstoppable in your quest for success if you have these tactics in your back pocket!

You may become so engrossed in a task that time becomes insignificant. Rather, it turns into a friend who helps you complete tasks and generates the best work possible. You can learn to harness time's power and use it to your advantage rather than against you with persistence and effort. Now, dive into this chapter as we journey towards improved time management and sharper focus.

Adjust How You See Time

Imagine having many things to accomplish when you get up in the morning and being determined to do each with vigor. However, as the day wears on, you discover that it becomes harder to remain concentrated and that you cannot determine how long each activity will take. Before you know it, half of your tasks are still unfinished, and it's late afternoon. For people with ADHD, this is the reality of time blindness, and I can personally identify with this problem.

It can be challenging to convey to others why it annoys you when you can't keep exact time. That's why having a support network that comprehends time management and can provide useful time management techniques is critical. It has nothing to do with laziness or lack of inspiration; rather, it has to do with difficulties in executive functioning and a distorted sense of time.

I've discovered techniques that have assisted me in overcoming time blindness by trial and error. One tactic I especially like is segmenting more complex projects into manageable steps. I can stay motivated and focused since I can observe little steps towards improvement.

Using visual tools to help me organize my time, such as color-coded calendars or timers, has also proven beneficial. Seeing time on a physical screen helps me better predict how long a task will take and adjust my schedule accordingly.

It's critical to remember that time blindness is an ADHD symptom, not a sign of character flaws. People with ADHD can conquer their condition with the right kind of assistance, techniques, medicine, and therapy.

Time Theft: The Effects Of Postponement

Let procrastination be your time thief. Even though you know what needs to be done, you simply can't bring yourself to do it. If you put off starting, restarting later will be more difficult. However, procrastination isn't always bad—there are instances when it might benefit us. For instance, we may put off tasks to rest or concentrate on other things first when we're exhausted or overly busy. But procrastination can become a problem if it keeps us from finishing vital chores and living life to the fullest! We'll examine the causes of procrastination in this chapter and strategies for overcoming it, such as setting daily goals and sprints and avoiding environmental distractions like cell phones.

Procrastination: A self-control issue

Self-control is required to overcome procrastination. Put differently, people who procrastinate are not lazy; they are just unable to control their actions.

Being able to manage your urges and complete things that need to be done is known as self-regulation. This involves putting off tasks until later (procrastination) and using impulse control to avoid temptations that prevent you from achieving your objectives.

You may master the skill of self-regulation at any age! You may do more with less effort by learning how to better manage your time and energy with practice.

The "why" behind putting things off

You and everyone else who procrastinates do it for the same reason. You believe things will improve, and the task won't be as difficult if you wait.

Sometimes, having a different attitude or having less on our minds makes things simpler. It is also true, though, that if we put off doing something, it will take longer later—and even longer if we keep putting it off until a later date. We can finish a task faster if we start early enough. This frees up time for other projects and reduces the chance of distraction.

There is no excuse for procrastinating other than laziness or lack of drive due to the law of diminishing returns, which states that delaying an action causes its effect to weaken with time. "I can't get started because I feel overwhelmed" or "I'm not motivated enough" are some things you can tell yourself. However, thinking this way makes things worse because it only gives us an excuse not to start and makes us feel horrible about ourselves when things don't go as planned!

Perfectionism and procrastination

Perfectionism is a cognitive distortion characterized by an excessively high self-improvement standard. "If I can do everything perfectly and make no mistakes, then I'll be worthy of love and respect," is the mentality that underlies perfectionism. However, that isn't how it operates!

Meeting those expectations may cause you to put off tasks because you believe you need more time or assistance than is now available. Or perhaps you just give up on trying because it seems too difficult and frightening. In either case, tension, worry, sadness, and even eating disorders can result from this pattern (particularly when the task at hand involves food).

Because we are always comparing ourselves to those who seem to be better than us at everything—even though they might not be—perfectionism can also lead to low self-esteem because nothing we achieve is ever truly great enough in our view.

www.ingramcontent.com/pod-product-compliance
Lightning Source LLC
Chambersburg PA
CBHW052149110526
44591CB00012B/1910